11/3
13/3

One Boy from Kosovo

For Annie and Andrea

With many thanks to Nutene Mehmetaj, the Nimani family,
Gerry Martone, David Arnold, Pashke Sinishtaj, and,
of course, Susan Pearson

One Boy from Kosovo
Text copyright © 2000 by Trish Marx
Photographs copyright © 2000 by Cindy Karp
Printed in the United States of America. All rights reserved.
http://www.harperchildrens.com

Library of Congress Cataloging-in-Publication Data
Marx, Trish.
One boy from Kosovo/by Trish Marx; photographs by Cindy Karp.
p. cm.
Summary: Tells the story of Edi Fejzullahu and his family, Albanians who fled their
home in Kosovo to live in a Macedonian refugee camp when the Serbs adopted a
policy of ethnic cleansing against Albanians.
ISBN 0-688-17732-8 (trade)—ISBN 0-688-17733-6 (library)
1. Kosovo (Serbia)—History—Civil War, 1998– —Refugees—Juvenile literature.
2. Refugees—Yugoslavia—Kosovo (Serbia)—Juvenile literature. 3. Albanians—
Yugoslavia—Kosovo (Serbia)—Juvenile literature. [1. Kosovo (Serbia)—History—
Civil War, 1998– 2. Refugees—Yugoslavia—Kosovo (Serbia) 3. Albanians—
Yugoslavia—Kosovo (Serbia)] I. Karp, Cindy, ill. II. Title.
DR2087.M37 2000   305.9′0691—dc21   99-051793

Typography by Michele Liebler
1 2 3 4 5 6 7 8 9 10
❖
First Edition

TRISH MARX

ONE BOY FROM KOSOVO

Photographs by

CINDY KARP

 HarperCollins*Publishers*

Cindy Karp, Edi, and Trish Marx at the Brazda refugee camp in Macedonia

AUTHOR'S NOTE

Cindy arrived in Stankovac 1 (STAN ko vich 1), commonly called Brazda, (BRAZ da), before I did. She had gone ahead to Brazda, a refugee camp in Macedonia, to find a child who was willing to be photographed and who would be able to share his or her story. When I caught up with her, a few days later, she had found Edmond Fejzullahu (FEZ you lah)—smart, handsome, funny Edi (ED dy), who had the leadership qualities of an entrepreneur and a well of sadness far beyond his years. It took Edi two days to decide to participate in the project. He was worried that somehow, by telling his story, his cousin and best friend Shkurta (SHOO ta), who was back in Kosovo, would be harmed by the Serbian soldiers. Edi's fear stemmed from the stories of torture and retaliation he and his family had heard daily—a friend was killed because she waved to the NATO planes; a house was burned because there was a picture of an Albanian leader on the wall. But ultimately, Edi felt it was important to tell his story so that other children around the world would know what it was like to live as a refugee.

And so for days, a woman with a camera and another with a tape recorder followed Edi around, sharing his meals, sleeping in his family's tent, meeting his friends. Sometimes telling the story was painful for Edi. But he would remind himself that he had made a contract, and go on. To Edi, his verbal agreement with us was a binding obligation to see the job through.

Now it is our turn to fulfill *our* contract with Edi, and with all the children of Brazda, by telling their story.

—Trish Marx
September 9, 1999

Albanian children and NATO peacekeepers at Brazda make the peace sign—expressing something they all hope for.

ABOUT KOSOVO

Serbs regard Kosovo as the cradle of their civilization and an important symbol of Slavic pride. Albanians believe they are descended from the ancient Ilyrians who first settled Kosovo. Both cultures feel they have a right to the same land. However, approximately 90 percent of the people living in Kosovo originally came from Albania, and only 10 percent originally came from Serbia. The ethnic tension is further aggravated by religious differences. Kosovar Albanians are Muslims, while the Serbs are mostly Orthodox Christians. The Albanians and Serbs speak different languages, but they have a shared history. Most of the Balkan Peninsula, which includes these countries, was ruled by the Ottoman Turks for over four centuries.

Boundary lines in the Balkans have been redrawn numerous times during the twentieth century. Kosovo became a province of the young Serbian nation in 1913, but the Albanian population has always chafed under Serbian rule. The Kosovars were allowed to rule themselves in a limited way after the Second World War, when Serbia and five other Balkan countries joined together to form a new Communist republic, Yugoslavia. A new Yugoslavian constitution granted Kosovo further powers of self-rule in 1974.

In 1987, Slobodan Milosevic became the president of the Serbian republic, within Yugoslavia. This new leader

The Federal Republic of Yugoslavia, as it was in the spring of 1999

1

advocated national unity and expansionism. He revoked Kosovo's partial independence, or autonomy, in 1989 and began systematically to deprive the Albanians of civil rights. Yugoslavia broke apart in 1991, shortly after the Soviet Union dissolved. Serbia and Montenegro declared a new, smaller Yugoslavian federation in 1992, with Milosevic as its president. Shortly thereafter, Serbia placed Kosovo under virtual martial law.

Milosevic's Serbian government closed down the high schools and universities that taught the language and history of Albania, and they also closed Albanian hospitals and news organizations. Only primary schools were allowed to teach in the Albanian language. Albanians had trouble getting visas to travel outside of Kosovo.

The plastic bottles on top of the tent are full of water being heated by the sun, for washing clothes and dishes. Shower water was also heated by solar power at Brazda.

They were forbidden to buy or sell property without special permission. The Albanian Academy of Arts and Sciences was closed. Albanian children could not use the same bathrooms as Serbian children. These began as temporary restrictions, but quickly became the law. In 1998 the Serbs, under Milosevic, instituted a campaign of ethnic cleansing against the Albanians. Serbian soldiers claimed that they were cracking down on the armed Albanian resistance group called the Kosovo Liberation Army. Kosovar Albanians went to war with the Serbs to protect themselves and to make Kosovo an independent state.

Shortly before hostilities broke out, the new Yugoslavia had joined the North Atlantic Treaty Organization (NATO). This was a group of North American and European nations that had agreed to protect one another in time of war. If one NATO country was attacked, the others would come to its defense. NATO worked toward a peaceful resolution of the conflict, but soon it became clear that Serbia would not cooperate. On March 23, 1999, NATO ordered a series of air strikes against strategic targets in Serbia and Kosovo. Seventy-nine days later, on June 10, the Serbian government announced that they would withdraw their troops from Kosovo. A United Nations international peacekeeping force moved in to help restore law and order in Kosovo on June 17, 1999. Fearing reprisals from the Albanians for atrocities committed during the war, many Kosovar Serbs fled their homes, becoming refugees in turn.

Children at Brazda played the same games they played at home, only with a new group of friends.

In the UNHCR compound, relief agencies distributed clothing donated from around the world. Some refugees had been forced to leave Kosovo with only the clothes on their backs.

During the war, almost one million Kosovar Albanians fled to other countries. Most of them went to one of the nine refugee camps in Macedonia that were run by the United Nations High Commissioner for Refugees (UNHCR). Other relief organizations, including Catholic Relief Services, the International Rescue Committee, and CARE, helped manage the camps. Shortly after the war ended, the camps emptied out and were closed.

Refuge means shelter, protection, or a safe place, and that is what the refugee camps were—a place of safety and protection for people who fled their homes and their country during a time of conflict.

THIS IS WHAT HAPPENED TO ONE BOY FROM KOSOVO IN THE SPRING OF HIS TWELFTH YEAR. HIS NAME IS EDMOND FEJZULLAHU, BUT HE IS CALLED EDI.

Edi grew up in Gnjilane (ju LANE), the third largest city in Kosovo, a province at the southernmost tip of Serbia. He has a mother and a father, an older sister and an older brother, many relatives, and many more friends. All his life, he lived in a large two-story house with four separate apartments. Edi's family lived in one apartment, and his father's three brothers lived in the other three, with their families. All the families pitched in to take care of the garden, and Edi's father and uncles shared a car. Edi had most things he needed, but because he was an ethnic Albanian living in Serbia, there were some things he could not do.

The things he could do seemed wonderful to Edi. He went to school every day with his cousin and best friend, Shkurta, who is three days younger than he is. He played sports, and he kept a journal. He celebrated his twelfth birthday with his friends and let Shkurta blow out the candles on a cake made with apples, strawberries, and oranges. He snuggled with his mother and laughed at his father's jokes. Edi was proud of being a Kosovar and felt safe in a happy home surrounded by loving relatives.

The Fejzullahu family: Sherif (father), Linda (age 17), Edi (age 12), Nexhmije (mother), and Shpend (age 14).

Edi's father was the head of the labor union for energy workers, but because he is an Albanian, the Serbian government had not paid him a salary for ten years. His mother was a schoolteacher, but she is also an Albanian, so she was not allowed to teach in the Serbian-run schools. Serbian and Albanian children attended school together until upper school, when Serbian children went on to high schools run by the government. Albanian children weren't allowed to attend these schools, so Albanian teachers taught them in private homes. Because these teachers were paid very little, Edi's mother decided to work as a hairdresser to help support her family.

Edi wanted to have a bicycle and a computer of his own, but his family could not afford to buy these things for him. Edi was still young enough to be in school with both Albanian and Serbian children, but his school did not have a computer. He had read about computers, though, and he hoped to be a computer programmer when he grew up. Edi would "dream with his eyes open," or daydream, about all the things he could do with a computer. He hoped that, if he did well in school, when he grew older he

Edi brought his school picture to Brazda to remind him of his friends at home. His best friend and cousin, Shkurta, is standing next to Edi in the second row.

Many refugees in the camp kept busy with the same kind of work they had done in Kosovo. Edi's mother gave haircuts to family and friends.

In the spring of 1999, about one million people—more than half the Albanian population of Kosovo—fled their country. Most went to refugee camps in Macedonia and Albania.

would be able to have one. He tried not to let the troubles between the Albanians and the Serbs in his country frighten him into not doing well in school.

Then everything changed for Edi and his family. March 1999 brought terror to Kosovo. The Serbian government in Belgrade had begun to encourage ethnic cleansing, which meant that they wanted only Serbs to live in all parts of Serbia—including Kosovo. In a concentrated effort to rid Kosovo of Albanians, the Serbian government sent tanks to block the main roads in many towns and villages in Kosovo. Soldiers, and civilians acting as soldiers, followed, knocking on the doors of Albanian homes, shouting to the people inside to leave immediately or be shot. Frightened Albanians grabbed a few possessions—a warm jacket, a photo album, whatever money they could find—then fled into the streets. They left televisions, computers, clothing, medicine, favorite heirlooms, and family pets. Some left their front doors open.

Almost one million Kosovars were forced to leave their country, shoved on crowded train cars and in the backs of trucks. Many families were separated.

7

Many families were separated at the Macedonian border. Hundreds of children were loaded onto buses headed to different refugee camps from their parents.

Some people fled under their own power. They went in cars and on buses. Anything with wheels was pressed into service, even farm equipment. Many of the Albanians who remained in Kosovo slept fully dressed so that they would be ready if the Serbs came to force them from their homes in the middle of the night.

Edi's family had heard about the ethnic cleansing, but they did not want to leave the home they loved. Then Edi's father came home with the terrible news that Serbian soldiers had killed one of his coworkers, along with ten members of the man's family. Like Edi's father, this man had held a position of leadership in the energy workers' union. Now Edi's father worried that the soldiers would come for him, too.

There seemed to be violence everywhere. Edi's mother heard that Serbian soldiers had shot a friend's daughter on the street when she ran out to look at a plane flying overhead. Edi's parents decided that they must leave their home.

Preparations were made quickly and in secret. They could only bring what they could carry—a few clothes and prized possessions. Edi's mother packed her scissors and cape for cutting hair, and she wore the small gold earrings her brother had given her. Edi's father brought his money belt and the orange notebook and pen he carried everywhere. Linda packed pictures from the family album, her journals in which she had written about her feelings and observations about the war, and her report cards. Shpend (Sh PEND) brought his class picture. Edi just wanted to bring his cousin Shkurta, but her parents had decided their family was staying in Kosovo. So he brought their class picture to remind him of her.

For a few weeks, Edi's family hid with relatives in Gnjilane and surrounding villages. They felt safer, but Edi's father always slept in a different house. He did not want the soldiers to find his wife and children with him. He feared they would all be killed, like his coworker's family.

One day, Serbian troops with guns and masks marched into the street where Edi was staying with his mother and brother and sister. It was the final straw for Edi's parents. They did not want to live in constant danger any longer. They told the children that if they went to a refugee camp, they would be safe. They would not really be refugees, they would just live like refugees for a little while. And as soon as they could, they would return to their life in Gnjilane. As thousands of other Kosovar Albanians had done, the Fejzullahu family would seek safety over the mountains, in Macedonia, a country south of Kosovo.

On a quiet, clear morning, the five of them walked to the crowded bus station. There were Serbian soldiers there. Edi clutched his father's hand. Linda walked with her head down. She had heard of young girls being raped by the soldiers. She was also worried that the soldiers would search the luggage and find her journals, which contained accounts of massacres and persecution in Kosovo. Edi and Shpend were scared, too. There were rumors that Serbian troops kidnapped young boys. The family huddled close to one another, fearful that they might be herded onto different buses going to different camps.

The Fejzullahus boarded their bus without incident, but they realized they weren't safe yet. Everyone had heard stories about people being taken off buses to be tortured or killed. Edi's mother told the children that if soldiers took their father off the bus, they were not to cry or complain or act

scared. If the soldiers took him, they would immediately get off the bus and go to hide in the mountains rather than be captured by the Serbians.

The family rode on the bus for many hours. Edi's legs cramped up, and he was hungry. Suddenly the bus stopped. Edi looked out the window and saw Serbian soldiers at a roadblock. Ahead of them were two more buses filled with refugees. Edi watched as soldiers boarded the first two buses, searching people and taking their money and jewelry. Then the soldiers boarded Edi's bus. Edi wished he were like the baby across the aisle, peacefully asleep on his mother's lap during this frightening time. He tried to remember what his mother had told him. Do not cry. Do not panic. He had never in his life been so

As soon as a busload of refugees arrived at Brazda, relief workers would hand water to the thirsty passengers.

9

scared. Suddenly, they heard the loud thunder of a bomb exploding and the hum of an airplane engine. The frightened Serb soldiers ran off the bus and drove away. Linda lifted her head off her lap, and Edi stopped clutching his father's hand. They realized they had been very lucky.

The bus reached the Kosovo-Macedonia border late in the afternoon. Everywhere Edi looked there were tanks, Serbian policemen, and lines of abandoned red tractors. Hundreds of farmers had fled on their only means of transportation—the bright red tractors they used to plant and harvest their fields. The tractors were the most valuable possessions the refugees owned, but they had been forced to leave them at the border. Edi heard people talking all around him. Would the border police let them through? Would the children be safe? Would families be separated? Someone even suggested they should get on another bus and go back home. Edi was too tired to listen anymore. He sat on his suitcase and waited.

There were hundreds of refugees entering Macedonia that night. Each person had to show identification papers. It took a long time for the immigration agents to read the names and addresses of so many people, to make sure they were who they said they were. The Macedonians were trying to prevent poverty-stricken people who were not refugees from sneaking into a camp, for the food

and shelter there. Seven hours later, at midnight, the family finally passed all the border checks.

The Fejzullahus didn't go directly to their refugee camp. Edi's mother had an uncle, Sedat (SEE dat), who lived in Macedonia close to the camps, and the family went to see him first. Edi's mother was worried about her younger brother, Kamber (CUM ber). She had not heard from him in weeks and hoped that their uncle might have news.

Sedat had a small house on a hill and a lovely garden. While they were there, Edi slept on the front porch. He liked to look at the river of lights coming from the city of Skopje (SKO pyeh) in the valley below. But the house was too small to hold five extra people for long. There was no news of Kamber, and after two weeks, the Fejzullahus went to join Edi's Aunt Sanije (SAN ieh) at the Brazda refugee camp.

Brazda was very different from anything Edi had ever seen. It was a huge tent city, erected on an abandoned airstrip and spreading into the surrounding fields. The entire camp was enclosed with a high wire fence. Macedonian police patrolled the fence and guarded the single entrance. Refugees, visitors, and relief workers carrying food and medicine poured by the busload through a large gate. A wide dusty road ran through the camp, with small shops selling soda and ice cream on either side of it.

The sprawling tent city Stankovac 1, also called Brazda, housed close to 30,000 people when Edi and his family lived there.

It's hard to keep a tent full of people clean with no running water. Aunt Sanije insisted everyone leave their shoes at the door so they wouldn't track dirt inside.

Edi saw some children climbing on an old airplane; others played basketball at a hoop stuck in the dry ground. Some of the people walking by were carrying loaves of bread, and all ages were mixed in together—old women wearing dimit (dee MEET), traditional divided skirts, were next to teenagers in jeans and T-shirts. Beyond the road, all he could see were tents, rows and rows of tents. Near the center of the camp there was a fenced compound of tents for the United Nations High Commissioner for Refugees (UNHCR) and the other groups responsible for running Brazda. These were the offices for administering the camp's food and water, garbage pickup, and health services—sort of a tent city hall. There were long lines of refugees in front of the service tents.

The Fejzullahus' bus stopped in the UNHCR compound. A relief worker looked over their papers and consulted a long list until he found Aunt Sanije's name and the number of her tent. Fortunately, there was room for Edi's family in the same tent. The relief worker gave each of them an emergency packet of soap, a toothbrush, shampoo, and a few other essentials and told Edi's father where to pick up the ration books that entitled the family to meals from the food tent. Then he led them down a narrow path between the tents to a large green one with laundry hanging from the sides. Many pairs of shoes sat by the front flap. A baby cried inside.

Aunt Sanije stepped out of the tent, crying out, *"Sije"* (SI yay: hello). She told them how lucky they were to be in this tent: There were cots to sleep on.

Inside the tent it was very dark and hot. A little girl with large brown eyes stared at Edi as he put his suitcase beneath an empty cot. He was grateful when Aunt Sanije told him there was a small room in the back of the tent for changing clothes, but he felt too tired to move. Edi's mother spread a blanket on his cot and told him to lie down. She said that he could brush his teeth tomorrow; there would be time for everything then. It was only early evening, but Edi fell asleep before he could say *naten e mire* (NAH ten ah mir: good night).

Over the next few weeks, Edi learned about living in a refugee camp. There was a line for everything: using the wood-and-canvas toilets set on the edge of the camp; taking a shower in a canvas shower stall, with water that had been warmed by the sun; and filling the plastic jugs with water from the row of metal spigots that supplied the whole camp. Brazda was intended to house twenty thousand people, but there were close to thirty thousand people living there. It seemed to Edi that he was either standing in a line, with nothing to do but wait, or sitting in his tent, with nothing to do but wait.

There was always a long line at the food tent. Edi's father stood in it several times a day to fill their canvas grocery bags with fresh bread, tomatoes,

Cots were the only furniture in the tents at Brazda. Edi and his parents made a cot platform so that the family could sleep and sit together.

13

Edi and his father had to wait in line several times a day to exchange ration coupons for fresh food. Lines were shorter at the stores that lined the camp's main road, but food there was very expensive.

cucumbers, peppers, canned fish, and containers of juice. It was all charged against the food ration book. One morning he came back with tiny dry sticks of bread. Nobody could tell him what they were, but the family ate them with fresh peaches for breakfast. Edi thought of the *burek* (BUR ik) he often had for breakfast at home, and he could almost taste the fried bread filled with spinach or cheese. He and Shkurta used to eat it on the way to school, but Edi

wondered now if he would ever taste it again.

Almost every evening, Edi's mother made the same simple dish of peppers, onions, and eggs over the small burner she had bought while they were staying with her uncle. Although the family got tired of eating the same thing every day, they were grateful they had hot meals. Most refugees had to make do with cold food. When someone got a special treat, such as a cake from a visiting relative, it was

Every morning Edi had to fill his water bucket from the outdoor spigots so that his mother could make coffee.

there was another tent just for dispensing medicine. Medical people put signs up urging people to be careful of sunburn, and to check themselves for lice. Aunt Sanije, who had been a nurse in Gnjilane, washed the floor of their tent every day with an antiseptic solution she had brought with her.

Near the center of the camp, by the compound that held the tents for the relief organizations, there was a large glass-enclosed bulletin board. This bulletin board was one of the few means of finding out

Heating food in the tent was tricky and dangerous, but even under these conditions, Edi and his mother enjoyed cooking together.

shared with everyone in the tent. The small girl with the large brown eyes ate hers so daintily that she had been nicknamed Princess.

Edi's mother was very careful with the burner when she cooked. The hot dry winds that blew through the camp all day long worried both refugees and relief workers—if a fire started in the camp, it would spread quickly from tent to tent. Another danger in the camp was disease. All garbage was immediately put in large cans that were emptied once a day into a yellow garbage truck. Two field hospitals were set up in the camp, and information about missing relatives. Pictures of lost people, often children, were posted on the bulletin board, in hopes that someone would recognize them. Pictures of refugees from other camps in the area were put up, too. Often families got separated at the Macedonian border and, in the confusion, were sent to several different camps. Many reunions took place because of the pictures on the bulletin boards. It was the refugees' lifeline, and Edi checked it several times a day to see if, just maybe, a picture of Uncle Kamber was posted on it.

Edi's father checked the bulletin board every day, too. Many countries around the world responded to the crisis in Kosovo by inviting a certain number of refugees to be their temporary guests. Lists of people who had been granted visas were posted on the board. Edi and his family read the lists, looking for the names of friends, wondering what country they might like to go to if they couldn't go home. One day they thought they should go to England. Another day, they agreed they should go to Australia. Edi thought he might like to go to school in the United States, but

Jehona Aliu   5 vjet

Pictures of lost and orphaned children were circulated throughout the camps in hopes of locating their families.

The bulletin board—information center of Brazda.

Edi hated it when new friends left Brazda, but no one stayed there for long. Many Kosovars chose to start new lives in foreign countries rather than wait for the war to end.

what he really wanted was to go home to Kosovo.

One morning, Edi recognized a name on the visa lists. A new friend he had met in the camp would be leaving for Sweden the next day. There were tears as all the girl's friends huddled around her, writing down their addresses from back home. In Gnjilane, Edi had known everyone in his school. If a new student came, he was always the first to make friends. But at the camp, it was harder. It seemed that as soon as he made a friend, his or her family would emigrate to another country.

Each time a friend left, Edi wrote out his Gnjilane address. And each time he wrote it down, he wondered if he would ever be back home to get a letter. He wished he had an E-mail address to give, too. He thought that if he had an E-mail address, he could still stay connected to his friends scattered around the world—wherever he might live.

Every day new refugees arrived at the camp from Kosovo. Everyone ran to the buses as they stopped inside the UNHCR compound. As people got off the buses Edi searched the new faces carefully. He hoped that Shkurta would be there, or a teacher from his town, or Uncle Kamber. But there were only more strangers. Edi watched as camp volunteers handed cups of water to the thirsty people. The faces that stared back looked both exhausted and grateful. Many of the refugees had been traveling for days and, like Edi, had left almost everything they owned behind. Edi felt the heaviness of being a refugee most intensely as he watched the new busloads of tired people.

Edi's favorite place in Brazda was the children's center, a large area set up like a day camp. There he could just be a kid again. There were all kinds of activities and games to play. There was even a stage

Edi was a volunteer at the children's center. He led games, distributed supplies, and helped the younger children with arts and crafts. But sometimes he just played.

Some days it seemed as though all the children painted were pictures of home. Edi encouraged the children to talk about their pictures, and it seemed to make them feel better about being in a refugee camp.

where counselors put on silly shows for the children, or held contests for the best dancer or "Mr. Camp Brazda."

Edi often volunteered to help the little kids paint and draw. After they finished, Edi encouraged the children to talk about their pictures. One little girl drew a candle sitting by an open book. She told Edi that her family could not use electric lights to read at night, because they were afraid their house might be bombed. One of Edi's favorite pictures showed a house on a street shaded with trees and lined with *bozhur* (bo JUR), the red flowers that symbolize Kosovar freedom. The young artist told Edi it was a picture of home.

As spring turned to summer, the weather grew hot and dry. The hottest time of the day was after lunch.

19

There were no trees in the camp for shade, and no streams to splash and swim in. Edi would relax on his cot. Sometimes he read to Princess from a book someone had left at the camp. Most days he ignored the heat and the chatter of the younger children in the tent and used this time to write in his journal, or to nap.

The summer heat made it hard to keep things clean. Everywhere Edi looked, there was laundry hanging on lines, or laundry put on the top of tents to dry, or women washing even more laundry. Small children were washed in the tubs, too. Everything in the camp was dusty, since all the roads were unpaved. Not long before, during the spring rains, everything had been thick with mud. The mud had been so deep that people's shoes were sucked off

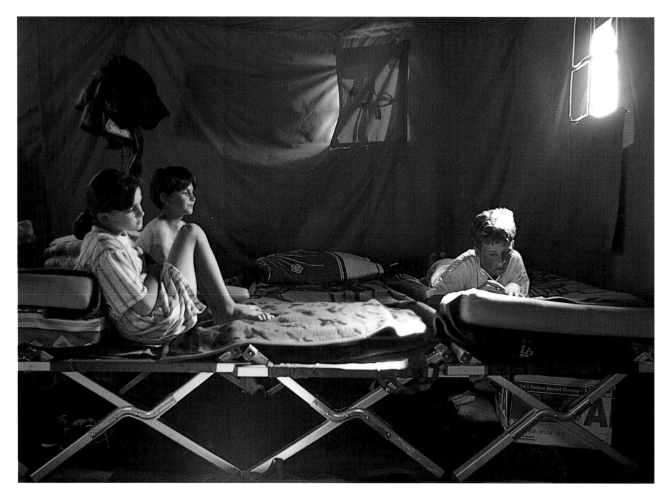

Boredom was one of the worst problems at Brazda, and people fought it in different ways. Linda and Edi recorded their thoughts and feelings in journals every day.

Edi and his father would unwind playing basketball.

their feet as they walked along the paths. Mud was in the food and on the blankets, and the rain that kept the mud coming was cold. Now, in summer, it was so hot and dusty that Edi had cut off his long jeans to make them more comfortable in the heat. Everyone said that the dust was better than the mud.

When the worst of the day's heat was over, people came out of their tents to stroll up and down the main road. Young people, especially, used this time of day to meet their friends and talk about home. Shpend would watch the Ping-Pong players as he waited for his turn. Edi and his father often joined a basketball game. There were no television sets, no movies, and no restaurants in the camp, but people found many ways to relieve their boredom and have some fun at the end of each day.

One evening, standing by the information board with his mother, Edi looked up to see several young men walking toward them. One of the men put his finger to his lips, telling Edi to stay quiet. But Edi let out a whoop and ran to the young man. He jumped into his arms and held tight. It was his Uncle Kamber! Kamber had walked over the mountains to reach the camp, hoping that some of his family would be there. Edi and his mother cried and cried and held Kamber tight.

After dinner, the family sat in their tent, drinking coffee and listening to Uncle Kamber tell how he had survived the past weeks. He had been in the mountains and had seen many families living there, drinking out of the streams and searching for food in the forests. These families were too afraid to stay in their towns and villages, but were not willing to leave their country.

When the cups were empty and fortunes had been told by pouring the coffee grounds into the saucer of each cup, the family took a walk in the cool of the evening. Except for the lights in the field hospitals, the camp was dark. The moon and the stars shone brightly. There was very little noise coming from the tents: a baby's cry, a burst of laughter, the murmur of soft voices, and then quiet again. Tonight Edi's family was together, and that was all that mattered for now.

Even though Edi was living in a refugee camp, there were some good times . . . like the day his Uncle Kamber arrived at Brazda.

EPILOGUE

Two months after the Fejzullahus entered Brazda refugee camp, the war ended, and Edi and his family went home to Gnjilane. Cindy and I heard from an American soldier stationed as part of the peacekeeping force in Gnjilane. Edi's mom had asked him to send us this E-mail:

Dear Cindy and Trish,

We are very happy for . . . the possibility to be in touch with you. No phone lines are working, and we are being in touch with you via the E-mail of this kind friend of ours. The time we spent together with you two is unforgettable. We hope you get the opportunity to visit us one day, otherwise we are all doing just fine and we are working thanks to God and Americans.